STUMBLING ON HISTORY

Other books by Fern Schumer Chapman

Is It Night or Day?

*Motherland: A Mother/Daughter Journey
to Reclaim the Past*

*Like Finding My Twin: How an Eighth-Grade Class
Reunited Two Holocaust Refugees*

STUMBLING ON HISTORY

AN ART PROJECT COMPELS A SMALL GERMAN TOWN TO FACE ITS PAST

FERN SCHUMER CHAPMAN

GUSSIE ROSE PRESS

Copyright © 2016 by Fern Schumer Chapman

Published April 1, 2017 by Gussie Rose Press, Lake Bluff, Illinois

Book and cover design by Tom Greensfelder

Printed by 1010 Printing Group Limited, China

Hardcover: ISBN 978-0-9964725-2-4   Paperback: ISBN 978-0-9964725-1-7

Library of Congress Cataloging in Publication Data

Chapman, Fern Schumer

Stumbling on History: An Art Project Compels a Small German Town to Confront Its Past
by Fern Schumer Chapman

1. Stolpersteine - Jewish - Non-fiction 2. Stumbling Stones - Germany 3. Activist Art Project -
Germany - Stolpersteine 4. Reconciliation - Social Aspects - Germany - History 5. Memory -
Social Aspects - Germany - History 6. Atonement - Social Aspects - Germany - Holocaust

10 9 8 7 6 5 4 3 2 1

To order additional copies of *Stumbling on History,*
go online to www.karben.com

For my husband, Bruce Jay Wasser,
who, as a teacher, inspired his students to strive for justice

FELLOW CITIZENS, WE CANNOT
ESCAPE HISTORY... THE FIERY
TRIAL THROUGH WHICH WE PASS
WILL LIGHT US DOWN, IN
HONOR OR DISHONOR, TO THE
LATEST GENERATION.

ABRAHAM LINCOLN
DECEMBER 1, 1862

HOW WE REMEMBER DETERMINES WHO WE ARE

We cannot escape history; it follows our every step, casting its shadow over our daily lives. "The past is never dead," the great American novelist William Faulkner said. "It is not even past."

How we remember — not just *what* — shapes who we are. As individuals, we find it difficult, when conscience tells us we've done wrong, to face up, say we're sorry, and make amends. For an entire nation, it is even harder to take the blame and make things right. When people have committed terrible acts as a nation, how do they atone for those acts and face their victims? Who speaks for a nation in apologizing—even when not everyone is sorry? Whose job is it to honor the past? And when should history be put behind us?

The United States has not always accepted and addressed its past wrongs. Native Americans, for example, have never received any official apology for the U.S. government's actions against indigenous peoples. Even though the Constitution now forbids slavery while guaranteeing citizenship and voting rights for African Americans, the government has never formally acknowledged the evil of slavery and has offered few acts of atonement.

In Germany, World War II left the fallout of unimaginable crimes. Before and during the war, in an effort to make the entire society racially pure, Nazi Germany murdered at least eleven million people. Six million Jews and five million other victims — including gays, political prisoners, Roma (gypsies), and disabled people — perished in what is now called the Holocaust.

Right: A row of Stumbling Stones in Germany. Next page: Railroad tracks leading to the concentration camp at Auschwitz.

For decades the German government has struggled with this shocking legacy. How should this nation recognize and atone for mass murder? Germany has tried to compensate and honor the Nazis' victims in several ways, including offering money to Jewish victims and to Israel. Germany also has required students to study the Holocaust, assuring this never happens again. In recent years, as World War II memories fade, Germans have worked to keep them alive, both as an important part of the nation's history and as a lesson in human respect.

One unique public art project honoring individual Holocaust victims is called *Stolpersteine* — German for "Stumbling Stones." Installed in cities and towns all over Germany and throughout other European countries as well, the "stones" are small bronze plaques set into sidewalks near the homes of displaced and murdered victims. The plaques list the names, birth and death dates, and places where the victims fled or died (often in concentration camps). Some plaques honor one individual; others list entire families. These powerful little plaques confront Germans with their past sins and their communities' involvement in this horrific historical event.

WHO WILL REMEMBER?
NOVEMBER 9, 2014

"Who will remember?"

My 89-year-old mother, Edith Westerfeld Schumer, seems to be talking to her reflection in the airplane window. We're flying toward the sunrise as we make our way to Frankfurt, Germany, the city nearest her birthplace, Stockstadt am Rhein, a town so small it doesn't even appear on most maps. Two Jewish families lived among its 2,000 people in 1938, when my grandparents sent their daughter, all alone at the age of 12, to live with relatives in America. Edith never saw her parents again.

If she hadn't gone, Edith probably would have been murdered by the Nazis, like her parents. The loss has haunted her all her life.

Several times in recent years, my mother and I have traveled to the town our family called home for nearly 250 years. We've made friends with some Stockstadt residents, the children and grandchildren of families my mother knew as a child. Many of our German friends belong to an organization with a most unlikely name: The German Society to Preserve Jewish Culture. Motivated by powerful guilt over their nation's past, members of this group have taken the deeply personal step of getting to know individual Jews, mostly Holocaust survivors and their families.

"We're all getting older," my mother says now, referring to our German friends who range in age from 70 to 90. Several face serious health issues.

"They're old," she continues. "I'm old now, too." We both know, though we don't discuss it, that this will be her last journey to her motherland.

"*Who?*" She turns to me, her eyes burning. "Who will remember? Fifty or a hundred years from now, who will know *this* happened?"

Above: Edith Westerfeld Schumer speaks about her experience fleeing Nazi Germany at the Illinois Holocaust Museum and Education Center in Skokie, Illinois. Opposite page: Untended Jewish graveyard in Kirkut, Poland.

Edith's family, the Westerfelds, was one of two Jewish families who had lived in Stockstadt am Rhein since the early 1700s. The family blended easily into the life of the town and proudly saw themselves as German first and Jewish second.

But when the Nazis came to power, their rule was harsh and personal for young Edith. Laws restricting and isolating Jews affected every aspect of her world. As the only Jew in her class, she sat alone in a corner, hung her coat on a hook far from the others, and often was bullied by her classmates — and even the teacher.

Her sister, their two cousins, and Edith were the only children in town not allowed into the movie theater or the local swimming pool. The music teacher quit giving lessons to Jewish children. One by one, friends stopped speaking to them. Not one single person came to Edith's 11th birthday party.

Nazi laws restricting and isolating Jews affected every aspect of her world.

And then, in 1937, neighbors — people Edith's father, Siegmund, considered his "friends" — nearly beat him, a decorated World War I soldier, to death.

Siegmund and Edith's mother, Frieda, knew the family had to leave Germany, but they couldn't get the necessary documents for the entire family. To save her life, they sent Edith alone to America, promising they would follow.

Left, top to bottom: 1930s postcard of Stockstadt am Rhein. Eleven-year-old Edith and her 14-year-old sister, Betty, just days before Betty boarded a ship for America in 1937 to live with a foster family in Chicago. The last picture of Edith with her parents, taken just days before 12-year-old Edith boarded a ship for America in 1938.

Along with nine other children, ranging in age from 4 to 16, she boarded the cruise ship *Deutschland* on a cold, gray day in March, 1938. Each child wore a tag with an assigned number around his or her neck. That number served as a mailing address, identifying the child and his or her destination.

On board the ship, Edith sent her first postcard to her dear friend, Mina Lautenschläger. The Great Depression of the 1930s had hit Mina's family of nine hard, so the Lautenschlägers asked the Westerfelds if Mina, their eldest child, could live with them. She would do chores in exchange for room and board. But during the years Mina lived with the family, she became another daughter to Frieda and Siegmund and another sister to Edith.

Edith wrote: "My dear Mina, I don't have much time. They are calling me. Just wanted to send you heartfelt greetings and kisses. Your Edith."

After 10 days on rough seas, the children finally saw the Statue of Liberty in New York Harbor. Edith was going to Chicago, a place as foreign as the moon, to live with an aunt and uncle she had never met. Uncle Jack, her father's brother, had arrived in America as a young man, long before Hitler came to power. He had married an American, Aunt Mildred, who reluctantly agreed to provide a home for Edith.

Center photo: A Nazi guards a Jewish shop with a sign in the window that says, "Germans!… Do not buy from Jews!"
Right, top to bottom: Jewish children fleeing Nazi Germany without their parents. Edith wrote this postcard to Mina on board the Deutschland *in March,1938. Edith's dear friend Mina Lautenschläger, at 19, when she lived with the Westerfeld family.*

Signs outside German towns which had expelled their Jewish neighbors during the Nazi era.

In America, Edith didn't receive many letters from her parents because the Germans censored most international mail. Edith worried constantly; she couldn't understand why her parents didn't want her to stay with them in Germany. At times, she thought, "Did they send me away because they didn't love me?" Eventually, the letters stopped completely.

In Germany, Edith's parents felt trapped as the Nazi noose tightened. Little by little, they lost everything. The government shut down the family business and demanded that they give up their home to a Nazi family. Sent to live in a "Jew House" far from their town and forced to work in factories under terrible conditions and without pay, the Westerfelds lost hope.

Taken on trains to two different concentrations camps, Siegmund and Frieda died with no one to mourn them or give them a proper burial.

Eventually, Mina discovered what had happened, and she wrote Edith the devastating news of her parents' deaths. Mina found out that the Nazis had murdered the Westerfelds from a notice posted on a bulletin board in the town hall that proudly announced that the town had achieved Hitler's goal — "Stockstadt is now *Judenfrei*" — free of Jews.

The Nazis made Mina's life miserable, too. For her allegiance to the Westerfeld family, the Nazis identified her as

a "Jew by association." She refused to stand up for the Nazi national anthem, salute Hitler, or put a *Heil Hitler* sign in her window. Mina often would say, "I will not howl with those wolves."

For her beliefs, Nazis harassed, fined, and spat on her. The *Bürgermeister* (mayor) identified her as "politically undesirable," making it impossible for Mina to get a job. As a result, she fled Germany and became a displaced person — someone who is forced to leave his or her home country because of war, persecution, or natural disaster. After World War II, Mina returned to her country, married, and had a son, Jürgen. But she would never forget the Westerfelds.

Identified as a "Jew by association," Mina would say, "I will not howl with those wolves."

Mina would see Edith again in 1990. By that time, Mina lived in a tiny, isolated hamlet of five houses in the Odenwald Mountains. After the Nazi period, Mina refused to live in Stockstadt again. "I paid for my politics all of my life. I will never make peace with the people of Stockstadt," she told Edith. "And I will never forget what they did to your family… our family."

During their visit, Mina gave Edith a special gift. Fifty years earlier, before she left Germany, Mina went to see Frieda, who was about to move to a "Jew House." When she entered the Westerfeld home, Mina found Frieda desperately sorting through household items she could sell in order to have money to buy food. Frieda found a toy china tea set with gold and blue trim that Mina and Edith played with before Edith left for America. Remembering how the girls loved playing "tea set," Frieda gave Mina the teapot, cups, and creamer.

Above: 1955 photo in Stockstadt. Mina is standing in the window and her son, Jürgen, is second from right. Left: 1943 photograph of Mina Lautenschläger. Below: 1951 photograph of eight-year-old Jürgen Flügge (Mina's son).

During their reunion, Mina returned the precious old tea set to Edith. Mina could never forget how the Westerfelds loved her; they were a constant presence in her life. In fact, Jürgen once told Edith, "My mother talked so much about you that I knew more about the Westerfeld family than I knew about my own."

Mina was outraged that few of the Nazis were punished for their crimes. Even worse, few Germans ever spoke of what happened between 1933 and 1945. As Mina repeatedly said to Jürgen, "Everything was forgotten after the war."

Above: After 52 years, Edith (left) and Mina finally saw each other again in 1990. Right: For 50 years, Mina kept this tea set, hoping to see Edith again and return it to her.

STUMBLING STONES: AN ACTIVIST ARTIST INSISTS THAT GERMANS REMEMBER

Decades after the Holocaust, a German activist artist decided to challenge his country's faulty memory. In 1996, he launched the Stumbling Stones project, creating small bronze cobblestone memorials to individuals who were displaced, murdered, or survived persecution during the Holocaust.

Gunther Demnig, who was born in Berlin, developed the idea for the Stumbling Stones from another one of his projects. In 1990, he marked in chalk the route Cologne's gypsies took when the Nazis deported them in 1940. When he retraced the chalk lines three years later, an older woman told him, "There were no gypsies in our neighborhood." Demnig realized she didn't know that they had been her neighbors. He wanted to change that frightening historical amnesia.

He designed the Stumbling Stones to link the names of Holocaust victims with the places where they had lived. Other memorials are easy to avoid, he says, since, "once a year, some official lays a wreath."

Not everyone liked his idea. In fact, during the first six years of his project, Demnig fought officials and bureaucracies who argued against his proposed installations.

"You just have to do it," he says, "and then you can achieve more than you imagined."

The Stumbling Stones project has placed tens of thousands of markers in more than 1,000 cities and towns throughout France, Poland, Italy, Denmark, and Austria, as well as Germany. School classes, communities, and individuals make donations to cover the cost of 120 Euros (about $133) for each Stumbling Stone. Demnig's team embosses 450 Stumbling Stones each month with an individual victim's name, birthdate, and fate; Demnig does most of the installations himself, traveling the continent to lay each one personally by hand.

Above: Activist artist Gunter Demnig. Below: In 1990, Demnig marked in chalk the route Cologne's gypsies took when they were deported in the 1930s. Opposite: Students help Demnig wipe the Stumbling Stones at an installation.

Though the number of installations is small in the context of millions of deaths, the Stumbling Stones team has made a conscious decision not to expand production, as a way of rejecting the huge, often impersonal scale on which the Nazis committed mass murder. The project can't possibly memorialize each Holocaust victim; still, demand for the stones is so great that Demnig is fully booked for years to come. He will install stones as long as he can, and he has plans to ensure that the project continues after he's no longer able to work.

"This is a different way of teaching history," Demnig explains. "Students open books and read 'eleven million people,' and they can't imagine. It is an abstract figure. With the stones, these people come to life. Young people say they would have played with [the victims'] children and grandchildren." In many towns, students research the lives of those who are memorialized and make presentations at the installation ceremonies.

> **"This is a different way of teaching history. Students open books and read 'eleven million people,' and they can't imagine."**

"Stumbling Stones create a place of memory for people where there was nothing before," says Demnig. The stones, though not large, are easy to read, and they're placed prominently in walkways, not along the edges of sidewalks, because, as Demnig explains, "You must 'stumble' with your head and heart, not just your feet."

Yet, not everyone supports the Stumbling Stones project. Munich, Villingen-Schwenningen, and Pulheim are among the cities that opposed the stones. Some opponents think it's disrespectful to walk on a memorial.

Others don't like the implications of the project. In Germany, families generally hand down their homes from generation to generation. Some

Left: Demnig and schoolchildren at a Stumbling Stones installation. Opposite below: The local Stockstadt newspaper announces the unanimous vote to install Stumbling Stones in the town. The headline reads, "So far, five names are identified."

Stumbling Stones are embedded at the locations where victims worked, but most are placed in front of the former homes of Holocaust victims. These may suggest that the current occupants of the homes had Nazi ancestors who stole the home from Jewish owners. Such families try to hide this shameful history.

Even Stockstadt's *Bürgermeister* Thomas Raschel anticipated a bitter fight when, in April 2014, he asked the Town Council to consider the installation of Stumbling Stones in front of the Westerfelds' former home.

Above left: The Westerfelds, some of the town's earliest settlers, built their home in Stockstadt in 1721. In 1939, Nazis stole the Westerfeld family home. Above right: In the 1970s, the new owners demolished the old house and built this house and shop in its place.

Bislang stehen fünf Namen fest

GEMEINDEPARLAMENT Stockstädter beschließen einmütig Verlegung von Stolpersteinen gegen das Vergessen

STOCKSTADT. Auch in Stockstadt sollen zum Gedenken an die während des Nazi-Regimes deportierten jüdischen Mitbürger sogenannte Stolpersteine verlegt werden. Das hat die Gemeindevertretung am Dienstag beschlossen.

Wo Bürgermeister Thomas Raschel (CDU) im April noch eine kontroverse Diskussion erwartet hatte, übten sich seine Gemeindevertreter in Einigkeit. Keine

bestehend aus den Familien Westerfeld, Kahn und Gutjahr. Bislang hätten Nachforschungen des Fördervereins für jüdische Geschichte und Kultur im Kreis Groß-Gerau und des Stockstädter Heimatforschers Jörg Hartung fünf Menschen aus diesen Familien ermittelt, die in den Vernichtungslagern der Nationalsozialisten ermordet wurden.

Der Bürgermeister wies darauf hin, dass in einer kleinen Gemeinde wie Stockstadt noch ein Gefühl bestehe für Nachbar-

beitung der Vergangenheit zu beginnen, die Erkenntnisse daraus an die nächsten Generationen weiterzugeben - und sich künftig gegen Extremismus in jeder Form aufzulehnen.

Werner Schmidt (parteilos) wies darauf hin, dass für die Gemeindegremien die Meinung der überlebenden Angehörigen von maßgeblicher Bedeutung gewesen sei. Dass aus den USA Zustimmung signalisiert wurde, habe die Entscheidung zugunsten der Stolpersteine bestätigt. Für die Grünen hatte Brigitte Huber auf kontroverse Diskussionen innerhalb ihrer Fraktion hingewie-

THE SPEECH OF BÜRGERMEISTER THOMAS RASCHEL TO THE STOCKSTADT TOWN COUNCIL

Stockstadt am Rhein had a relatively small Jewish community. The survivors and descendants of the Westerfelds have explicitly expressed interest and agreed to the Stumbling Stones. The story of this family is well known, in part because of the literary work of the Westerfelds' granddaughter, Fern Schumer Chapman.

In her book, *Motherland: Beyond the Holocaust — A Mother/Daughter Journey to Reclaim the Past*, she tells the story of her and her mother's trip to Germany. In October 1990, Edith Westerfeld Schumer returned to the place where she was born. They visited Stockstadt am Rhein.

In 1938, her parents sent Edith Westerfeld, who was only 12, to live with relatives in America. The Nazis murdered her parents. The places where we want to install the Stumbling Stones make it clear that this barbarity also occurred in the middle of our community. Even here in our town on the Rhein, man fell victim to Nazi madness. We should therefore lay Stumbling Stones here.

Sorrow and joy are closely tied together in such an installation. Sadness, because it is horribly cruel to torture people because of their Jewish origin and kill them, and joy, because here, at this point, it is a long time ago, and we want to pay our respects to the victims.

Stumbling Stones are a remembrance and a reminder of that time. They are important for the whole family and our community. They should not be forgotten. We must remember each family member's specific features.

A good working memory is a prerequisite for the mastery of the present.

The memory of the victims also is a public responsibility. The almost forgotten private suffering of our missing neighbors can now be preserved in public; the silence will be broken about the past and the future can be designed jointly.

Our neighbors are gone forever through the pitfalls and the lack of public discussion. But now, the family name will be called again. In keeping with the Jewish tradition: "A person is only forgotten if his name is forgotten."

"Stumbling Stones are important for the victim's family and our community," the *Bürgermeister* told the Council in an impassioned speech. "This barbarity occurred in the middle of our community. Even here in our little town on the Rhein, man fell victim to Nazi madness.

Not one voice was raised against the resolution to lay Stumbling Stones in Stockstadt.

"The memory of the victims is a public responsibility," he continued. "Our neighbors are gone forever through the pitfalls and the lack of public discussion. But now [with the installation of Stumbling Stones], the family name will be called again. In keeping with the Jewish tradition: 'A person is only forgotten if his name is forgotten.'"

The Council voted to support the project. Not one voice was raised against the resolution to lay Stumbling Stones in Stockstadt.

When my mother read Thomas Raschel's eloquent speech, I noticed she didn't seem to be as moved as I was. She recalled that in 1938, the then-*Bürgermeister*, who lived directly across the street from her family, was Stockstadt's most prominent Nazi.

IN FRONT OF YOUR HOUSE, IN MEMORY OF YOUR FAMILY

There are no burial sites for those murdered during the Holocaust. The installation ceremony is an important memorial service, a kind of funeral for the victims, and the Stumbling Stones are remembrances of their lives.

But sadly, in some places, the ceremonies are not well-attended. Surviving members live in other countries, and it is difficult for them to travel to these events. In addition, many residents of the German towns prefer to forget the role their family or town played in Nazi crimes.

There are no burial sites for those murdered during the Holocaust.

The ceremony in Stockstadt, however, would be different. For hundreds of years, the Westerfeld family was prominent in the small town. My mother and I traveled to Stockstadt to witness this important event, and many German friends were planning to join us as well.

But my mother and I were sad to learn that Jürgen Flügge, the son of my mother's closest German friend, Mina, would not be among them. After his mother passed away at the age of 74 in 1992, Jürgen grew close to my mother and me. We treasured the memory of Mina, whose courage made her what Jews today call a "Righteous Gentile." Unfortunately, a few weeks before the Stockstadt installation, Jürgen underwent surgery and was recuperating in a rehabilitation center in a faraway town.

Now, on this overcast Saturday afternoon, November 15, 2014, my mother and I join a crowd of Stockstadt residents, waiting for the ceremony to begin. Surprisingly, more than 150 people pack the sidewalk in front of the former Westerfeld home, a crowd so large that it spills onto the main street, blocking traffic.

Above: Edith at the Stumbling Stones installation site, just steps away from what was once the front door of the Westerfeld home. Left: Nazis rounding up Jews in 1942 and marching them to a train in Pilsen, Czechoslovakia.

I scan the crowd for familiar faces, smiling and waving to several friends. Then, my gaze lands on a man standing next to a building, and I do a double-take. A large, bald-headed, well-dressed man is smiling broadly at me. My heart jumps!

But — are my eyes playing tricks on me? Squinting, then taking a few steps closer, I see it's really Jürgen! Leaving my mother's side, I run to him. "What are you doing here?" I gasp, hugging him as tightly as I can. Then, I step away and take a good look at his face. "Aren't you supposed to be in rehab?"

"I couldn't miss this," he says, smiling.

"Shouldn't you be in *rehab*?" I notice he's pale and thin, and I wonder whether Jürgen should be out of bed. "What did the doctors say?"

"Nothing," he says, shrugging his broad shoulders. "I didn't ask."

"You just *left*?" My voice and my eyebrows rise with alarm.

"I *had* to be here." Jürgen waves off my worries. "For you, your mom, and Mina."

> "I *had* to be here." Jürgen waves off my worries. "For you, your mom, and Mina."

We suspend our conversation, and I run back to the podium as the event begins. Wearing his traditional work clothes—felt hat, denim shirt, tan vest, old jeans—Gunter Demnig picks up his trowel and starts digging up the old cobblestones, mere steps from what was once the Westerfelds' front door. (The new owners tore down the original Westerfeld home and replaced it with a new house and shop.) As Demnig works, the *Bürgermeister* welcomes the audience and explains the significance of the stones. Several other local politicians offer a few words of welcome.

Left: Fern sees her old friend, Jürgen (Mina's son); Fern and Jürgen hug; Fern, Edith, and Jürgen at the installation of the Stumbling Stones in Stockstadt. Opposite left: Demnig digs out cobblestones to install Stumbling Stones for the Westerfeld family. Opposite right: Edith, the only remaining Westerfeld, speaks at the Stockstadt ceremony.

Then, the head of the German Society to Preserve Jewish Culture invites my mother, the only surviving member of the original Westerfeld family, to the podium. Edith looks small, still child-like, standing before the crowd. Yet, she finds her voice, and, with conviction, makes a brief statement.

"I'm glad to be with you today. Thank you for remembering my family.

"As you have just heard my story, I won't need to retell it today. Hatred has a long reach, especially in families of the victims. Sadly, what happened to me decades ago didn't simply disappear when I started a new life in America. It affected my life and my children's lives, so much that my daughter was moved to write books about the experience and its legacy.

"What's even more frightening is that anti-Jewish hatred is emerging once again, here and around the world. I am standing before you today, pleading with you to think

"What happened to me decades ago didn't simply disappear when I started a new life in America."

21

about your actions—from bullying in schoolyards to hateful acts on the streets. As the Nobel Peace Prize winner Elie Wiesel has said, 'All that is necessary for the triumph of evil is that good men do nothing.'

"It is up to you. You must do something. You must speak up to stop hatred. You never know: one day, it might be your family that becomes the victim."

My mother takes a seat in the front row as Jürgen steps up to the podium. This is a moment he has yearned for his entire life—a chance to speak directly to Stockstadt's residents for himself, his mother, Mina, and the Westerfelds.

"Dear Edith, Dear Fern: When we are standing here today together and thinking about the terrible injustices that happened to your family, we seem to use special words. We say that the families 'disappeared.' They didn't disappear. They were driven away. Or we refer to Jewish families as *mitbürghers*, while Germans are called *bürghers* or residents. In other words, Jews were not true residents, but someone who we allow to live among us Germans. Now we have Turkish *mitbürghers*.

"Your house was attacked and partly destroyed by Nazi gangs, people living across the street — like the mayor."

"But when I think about what happened during the Nazi time in Germany, especially in Stockstadt — one of the first towns to have Nazi activity — I think of Mina, who lived in your family home as a housekeeper. What would Mina say on this day of memory for your family?

"She would say, 'Finally! Finally!' It is 75 years after the beginning of Hitler's war and 76 years after the night your house was attacked and partly destroyed by Nazi gangs, mostly people living across the street like the mayor, *Bürgermeister* Metzger, and neighbors who lived right next door."

"Why would no one remember what happened between 1933 and 1945?"

Here, Jürgen points to the *Bürgermeister's* house. Following his finger, I'm startled to see a shadowy figure standing at the window, removed but watching the scene below, like a ghost.

"Finally," he continues, "a sign of remembrance.

"But Mina would ask, 'Why so late?' Maybe because all the Nazis in Stockstadt and the bystanders are dead—these people who did so much harm to your family.

"Everything was forgotten after the war. The new residents of your home forgot that they were the illegal owners. The town forgot what they had done 12 years before the war in Stockstadt. I found a suitcase that Mina had, and I have a list of all the Nazis here. I know who you are. Mina would ask, 'Why didn't other people help me when I went to the court to ask for your rights in the Westerfeld name? Why would no one remember, two years after the war, what happened between 1933 and 1945? I was standing alone. Was it repression? Was it lies? Were they ashamed to say something?' No.

"They only wanted to keep what they had stolen from the Jewish residents—the houses, the household goods, the synagogues, the art. This was the beginning of the new German Republic. This is what is called 'zero hour.' We have a new beginning and nothing before then happened.

"But history doesn't have a zero hour. We are linked to our history. A lot of Nazis dived into the

Opposite page: Speaking for his mother, Mina, who died in 1992, Jürgen reproaches residents about what Stockstadt's Nazis did to the Westerfeld family. Left: 1945 photograph of Mina as a young mother with her two-year-old son, Jürgen. Above: A Jewish home destroyed in 1938 in Ober-Ramstadt, near Stockstadt.

Above: Members of the Lutheran Church Choir perform two hymns at the conclusion of the ceremony.
Below: After Jürgen speaks, he embraces Edith.

---

new parties. They joined the conservative Christian Democratic Union. The boss of the new government's secret service was the boss of Hitler's secret service. A high-ranking Nazi became the State Secretary under the new Chancellor.

"'They are not gone,' Mina always said. 'They are still here.' Mina also would say, 'No revenge. Only justice.' She wanted a real memory and accounting of the terrible acts of these gangsters, and, even more important, remembrance of the victims. She wanted a memory of the pain that these so-called Christians caused Stockstadt's Jewish citizens.

"Never again should there be another government like the Nazi regime!

"Dear Edith, Dear Fern, Mina would be so happy to see you in front of *your* house because it is *your* house. She would be so happy to see us together here in front of *your* house in memory of *your* family that was also for a long time Mina's family. The time Mina lived with your family defined her whole life.

"Dear Edith, Dear Fern, we bow to you, your sister and aunt Betty, Frieda, Siegmund, and *Oma* [Grandmother] Sara. I thank you for your courage in coming here with open hearts and friendship."

No one stirred or said a word as Jürgen left the podium to embrace Edith. Many of the chastened witnesses hung their heads as the Lutheran Church Choir concluded the ceremony by performing two hymns — one Christian and one Jewish.

After the ceremony, witnesses placed white roses — symbolizing hope, freedom, and friendship — on the stones.

Witnesses placed white roses — symbolizing hope, freedom, and friendship — on the stones.

"WE'RE SORRY"

The Stumbling Stones program is the largest, most ubiquitous European Holocaust memorial, but other monuments are scattered in the area surrounding Stockstadt. These places of remembrance at crucial locations — the Darmstadt railroad tracks where Jews were deported, the location of a former synagogue in Gross-Gerau, even the restored synagogue in Erfelden — encourage reflection and dialogue. But the installation and ceremony of the Stumbling Stones in Stockstadt led to a particularly dramatic encounter for my mother and me.

After the ceremony, two leaders of Stockstadt's Lutheran parish — minister Christiane Seresse and her husband, vicar Marcus David — call our host, Christina Mager, and ask that we visit their 400-year-old church. The community held events there in the 1930s, they tell her, and they're eager to see if my mother remembers the décor.

The following morning, before leaving for the Frankfurt airport to fly home, we stop by the church for a few minutes. We enter, and as my mother looks around the beautiful little sanctuary with its fine stained-glass windows and bright light pouring into the pews, she observes, "You painted the dark wood white."

Christiane and she talk about the appearance of the church in the 1930s and how it has changed over the years. I look around and notice two lit candles flickering on the altar. Is there some other reason, I wonder, that the church leaders insisted we come here today?

Christiane breaks away from my mother and walks to the front of the sanctuary. Gesturing for us to take seats in a front pew, she picks up a guitar. "Before you leave," she says, "I'd like to send you off with a German song." Her sweet soprano voice fills the church as tears stream down her cheeks.

Mach mein Herz für andre Menschen weit,
lass mich werben für die Ewigkeit.
Lass mich leben, wo die Liebe wohnt,
und mit weitem Horizont.

Make my heart wide for other people,
let me woo for eternity.
Let me live where love resides,
with a wide horizon.

The synagogue in Erfelden that Edith attended. In recent years, Germans have restored local synagogues in many towns. Today, with no Jewish people living in the area, the building is used to bring back to the community what Jews contributed — arts and culture.

Church leaders Marcus David and Christiane Seresse with Edith and Fern.

As she finishes the song, struggling and swallowing hard, Christiane says, "I also want to read you a statement." Collecting herself, she begins, her voice shaking:

"Dear Mrs. Schumer, Dear Mrs. Schumer Chapman,

"This has been my favorite song in the last few weeks — a prayer for a wide horizon, a prayer for hope that jumps over walls, and for faith that moves mountains.

"Yesterday I found this prayer to be fulfilled. You came here to Stockstadt with a wide horizon and an open heart and did exactly this: you jumped over the wall of silence, you removed the mountain of alienation.

"It should have been *our* job to do so, because we were the ones who made your family outsiders. We were the ones who hurt your family incredibly and even took the lives of your parents and part of our own lives.

> "We were the ones who hurt your family incredibly and even took the lives of your parents."

"But you came back to Stockstadt with your friendly, open mind and conquered our hearts. You offered a new relationship to us and smoothed the way to reconciliation. This is a great gift for us, and I hope that the people of Stockstadt will take that chance.

"And I beg your pardon to forgive us that our church didn't protect you and your family, and that we didn't resist all the injury you suffered, I hope we will meet again. Let's keep in contact.

"Christiane Seresse, Marcus David"

Until this day, no one ever has directly acknowledged the betrayal and terrible losses my mother has endured. She has waited eight decades to hear these words. Now, at last, someone has come forward to deliver what she always felt she deserved.

An apology.

Stunned, my mother can't bring herself to respond to Christiane. Edith stares into the distance. Finally, she turns to Christiane and whispers, "Thank you. I appreciate your words."

My mother has one last request before we leave Stockstadt, her hometown, a place she may not see again. She wants to walk the short distance from the Lutheran Church to the site of her childhood home. Before we leave Germany, she wants one last look at her family's stones.

The glass memorial at the Darmstadt railroad tracks is inscribed with the names of those deported from this location to concentration camps, including Frieda and Siegmund Westerfeld.

This 1937 portrait is the last photograph of the Westerfeld family: Edith, Frieda, Siegmund, and Betty.

The stones look clean, shiny, and permanent. Mom examines them closely. The first line engraved on the stones states, *Hier wohnte,* "Here lived," and then come the names of each family member displaced or deported. The stones memorialize my mother's grandmother, Sara Westerfeld, who died from stress and humiliation on August 24, 1939; her father, Siegmund Westerfeld, who died in Sachsenhausen (Germany) concentration camp on February 15, 1942; her mother, Frieda Westerfeld, who was deported and died in a concentration camp in Piaski (Poland), on an unknown date in 1942; her sister, Betty Westerfeld Zwang, who fled to the United States in 1937, and the last survivor, Edith Westerfeld Schumer, who fled to the United States in 1938.

"All the people in Stockstadt — for all time — will know what happened here. They will see the Stumbling Stones."

"People come to the shop on summer evenings, buy ice cream, and then eat their cones at the chairs and tables here." Christiane says, pointing to a spot next to the stones — the same space in front of the old Westerfeld home where my mother played as a child. "It's a gathering place now."

"I promise you," Christiane continues, taking both of my mother's hands and looking directly into her eyes. "All the people in Stockstadt — for all time — will know what happened here.

"They will see the Stumbling Stones."

HIER WOHNTE
SARA
WESTERFELD
GEB. HERTZ
JG. 1860
GEDEMÜTIGT / ENTRECHTET
TOT 24.8.1939

HIER WOHNTE
SIEGMUND
WESTERFELD
JG. 1891
VERHAFTET 14.6.1941
SACHSENHAUSEN
ERMORDET 15.2.1942

HIER WOHNTE
FRIEDA
WESTERFELD
GEB. KAHN
JG. 1898
DEPORTIERT 1942
PIASKI
ERMORDET

HIER WOHNTE
BETTY
WESTERFELD
JG. 1922
FLUCHT 1937
USA

HIER WOHNTE
EDITH
WESTERFELD
JG. 1925
FLUCHT 1938
USA

COMING TO TERMS WITH
A NATION'S CRIMES

"What atonement is there for blood spilled upon the earth?"

More than two thousand years ago, the Greek writer Aeschylus posed the question of historical responsibility: how nations admit, remember, and atone for shameful acts.

Since he wrote those words, countries have spilled unimaginable quantities of blood upon the earth. Only in recent years have nations begun to recognize the need for historical responsibility about actions such as these — all committed worldwide, even in the present day, and many as yet unacknowledged:

- forced, often violent displacement of native peoples

- use of chemicals in warfare

- acts of racial discrimination and violence

- acts of religious intolerance

- acts of hatred, often violent, toward gay, lesbian, bisexual and transgender people

At the same time, however, some countries have taken responsibility for terrible acts in their past:

- In addition to financially compensating victims of the Holocaust, Germany has welcomed thousands of refugees from the Middle East, as part of its responsibility to humanity because of its past Nazi crimes.

- In 1988, the United States Congress approved a formal apology to more than 110,000 Japanese Americans who were removed from their homes and interned in camps during World War II. The government also awarded $20,000 to each person who had been interned.

- After Rwanda's bloody civil war in the 1980s, killers from both the Hutu and the Tutsi tribes sought forgiveness from their victims' families. This nationwide effort is considered a great success in helping the country heal.

- In 2008, the Australian government issued a formal apology to the "stolen generations" — Aboriginal and Torres Strait Islander children taken from their families and communities — for the suffering of these people, their families, and their descendants.

- In 2016, President Barack Obama acknowledged responsibility for the horrors unleashed by the world's first atom-bomb attack by visiting Hiroshima, Japan. He was the first sitting U.S. President to do so.

Like these examples, the Stumbling Stones project is an honorable effort to recognize and redress historical wrongs. It is necessary and important for both victims and perpetrators. In the perceptive words of the late Nobel laureate Elie Wiesel, carved at the entrance of the Holocaust Memorial Museum in Washington, D.C.: "For the dead and the living, we must bear witness."

PHOTO CREDITS

ACKNOWLEDGEMENTS

Thank you to my German friends who have worked tirelessly to ensure that communities in Hesse face their history and remember the Jewish neighbors who once lived among them: Christina Cornelia Mager, Irene and Gert Krell, Elfriede Marwitz, Angelika Borchert and Jürgen Flügge, Ulrich and Else Trumpold, Walter Ullrich, Ulf and Catarina Kluck, Ludwig Nösinger, Christiane Seresse and Marcus David, Margaret Wohlfahrt-Stoll, Tanja Kraft-Leichtweiss, and Christel Göttert.

Thank you to Karen Sloan Keane and Susan Rosen Sternberg, my American friends who made the trip to Germany to offer support to our family and witness the ceremony. I treasure their longstanding love and friendship… and their photos. I'm also delighted I had the opportunity to meet my own long-lost relatives — Wolf Bohlen, Christina Raihani, and Ruth Garstka — at the Stumbling Stones installation, and I'm grateful for their warm embrace.

My supporting cast once again came through for me. Designer Tom Greensfelder brought the story to life on the page with his keen eye and artistic sensibilities. My friend, award-winning author James B. Lieber, provided consistent encouragement of what he has labeled "the Edith Westerfeld saga." My editor and friend, Susan Figliulo, polished the copy with her usual fastidiousness.

Finally — always — I'm indebted to my mother, Edith Westerfeld Schumer, who continues to open herself up to the past through my writing. My brother, Scott Schumer, has walked beside me spiritually on this journey. My three children, Ross, Keith, and Isabelle Chapman, inspire me to strive to make the world a better place.

IF YOU ENJOYED **STUMBLING ON HISTORY,**
YOU'LL WANT TO READ THE COMPANION BOOK:

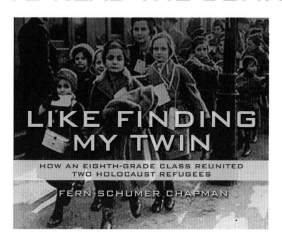

Every student should read it. Every school should teach it.

—Pulitzer Prize nominee James B. Lieber

On the ship that brought her from Nazi Germany to America, young Edith Westerfeld met Gerda Katz. Both 12-year-old girls were traveling alone and immediately became best friends. Unfortunately, the two unaccompanied minors lost touch after their arrival in 1938.

Decades later, after a northern Illinois middle-school class read *Is It Night or Day?* by Fern Schumer Chapman, a historical novel that captures the two girls' friendship, the students were so moved by the story that they made it a class project to reunite the two women.

Through photos, historical documents, and storytelling, *Like Finding My Twin* captures the friendship of the two Holocaust refugees, the students' research, and the remarkable reunion 73 years after Gerda and Edith shared their immigration journey.

To order copies, please visit www.karben.com

HIER WOHNTE **AMALIE BENDER** GEB. ROSENBAUM JG. 1902 DEPORTIERT 1942 PIASKI ???	HIER WOHNTE **FRANZISKA BRETZFELDER** GEB. STARK JG. 1894 FLUCHT IN DEN TOD 1.4.1942	HIER WOHNTE **LORE LUISE FELLHEIMER** JG. 1929 DEPORTIERT 1941 KAUNAS ERMORDET 25.11.1941	HIER WOHNTE **DR. EMIL NEUSTADT** JG. 1873 GEDEMÜTIGT / ENTRECHTET TOT 8.5.1937	HIER WOHNTE **KITTY NEUSTÄTTER** GEB. HERZ JG. 1902 DEPORTIERT 1941 KAUNAS ERMORDET 25.11.1941
HIER WOHNTE **GISELA 'GITTL' GOLDMANN** GEB. ULLMANN JG. 1863 DEPORTIERT 1942 THERESIENSTADT ERMORDET IN TREBLINKA	HIER WOHNTE **ALFRED FLEISCHMANN** JG. 1874 DEPORTIERT 1942 PIASKI ???	HIER WOHNTE **THERESE HÖNIGSBERGER** GEB. STERNFELD JG. 1866 VOR DEPORTATION FLUCHT IN DEN TOD 1.8.1942	HIER WOHNTE **ALFRED HÖNIGSBERGER** JG. 1858 DEPORTIERT 1942 THERESIENSTADT ERMORDET 12.7.1942	HIER WOHNTE **REGINA REBEKKA MEEROWICZ** GEB. WAINSCHEL JG. 1894 DEPORTIERT 20.11.1941 KAUNAS ERMORDET 25.11.1941
HIER WOHNTE **ARTHUR GRÜNEWALD** JG. 1887 DEPORTIERT 1943 ERMORDET IN AUSCHWITZ	HIER WOHNTE **JAKOB KAPHAN** JG. 1876 DEPORTIERT 1942 THERESIENSTADT ERMORDET 9.7.1944	HIER WOHNTE **ANNA GOTTSCHALK** JG. 1891 FLUCHT IN DEN TOD 14.11.1938	HIER WOHNTE **DOROTHEE GUTMANN** GEB. BÜCHENBACHER JG. 1901 DEPORTIERT 20.11.1941 ERMORDET 25.11.1941 KAUNAS	HIER WOHNTE **ROSA MITTEREDER** GEB. LOEWI JG. 1891 DEPORTIERT 1941 KAUNAS ERMORDET 25.11.1941
HIER WOHNTE **MARTHA GOLDSCHMIDT** GEB. KOCH JG. 1869 DEPORTIERT 1942 THERESIENSTADT ERMORDET 13.1.1945	HIER WOHNTE **EDUARD GOTTSCHALK** JG. 1883 FLUCHT IN DEN TOD 14.11.1938	HIER WOHNTE **RUBEN EINSTEIN** JG. 1930 DEPORTIERT 1943 ERMORDET IN AUSCHWITZ	HIER WOHNTE **HANS JOACHIM BRETZFELDER** JG. 1921 FLUCHT FRANKREICH DEPORTIERT 1942 ERMORDET IN AUSCHWITZ	HIER WOHNTE **OLGA NUSSBAUM** GEB. GUNDERSHEIMER JG. 1899 DEPORTIERT 1943 ERMORDET IN AUSCHWITZ
HIER WOHNTE **ELSBETH ENGELMANN** GEB. ROSENFELD JG. 1870 DEPORTIERT 1942 THERESIENSTADT ERMORDET IN	HIER WOHNTE **THERESE GUTTNER** GEB. GOLDSCHMITT JG. 1898 DEPORTIERT 1941 KAUNAS	HIER WOHNTE **HERMINE EBERSTADT** GEB. MASBACH JG. 1853 DEPORTIERT 1942 THERESIENSTADT	HIER WOHNTE **GERTRUD CAHN** JG. 1921 DEPORTIERT 20.11.1941 ERMORDET 25.11.1941 KAUNAS	HIER WOHNTE **GERTRUDE MASSER** GEB. HIRSCH JG. 1891 DEPORTIERT 1941 KAUNAS ERMORDET 25.11.1941